I AM NOT A CROOK!

Donald Gorbach

ISBN:1977605125
ISBN-13: 978-1977605122

"WHEN THE PRESIDENT DOES IT, THAT MEANS THAT IT
IS NOT ILLEGAL "

-RICHARD NIXON

www.ingramcontent.com/pod-product-compliance
Lightning Source LLC
Chambersburg PA
CBHW050911260726
48660CB00001B/148